The
Children's
MADIBA

PUFFIN BOOKS

The
Children's
MADIBA

The life story of
NELSON MANDELA

Sean Fraser
Illustrations by Tom Kyffin

First published by Puffin Books, South Africa, 2013
An imprint of Penguin Books (South Africa) (Pty) Ltd
A Penguin Random House company
Registered Offices: Block D, Rosebank Office Park, 181 Jan Smuts Avenue,
Parktown North, Johannesburg 2193, South Africa

www.penguinbooks.co.za

Reprinted 2013

ISBN 978-0-14-353852-3
e-ISBN 978-0-14-353115-9

Cover design by publicide
Cover illustration by Tom Kyffin
Design and typesetting by Tracey Fraser
Printed and bound by Ultra Litho

Once, not so long ago, in the small rural village of Mvezo tucked away among the rolling hills of the Eastern Cape, there lived a Xhosa chief and his four wives. The chief's name was Hendry Mandela. He loved all his wives and their children played happily together in the family kraal that was their home. Then, on 18 July 1918, Hendry's third wife, Fanny, gave birth to a baby boy. Hendry and Fanny were very happy, and named their youngest son Rolihlahla Mandela.

Little Rolihlahla had many brothers and sisters, and they were very excited about the new baby. As the cold winter began to fade and summer brought hot, sunny days, the baby grew into a happy and healthy boy. The family moved from Mvezo to the nearby village of Qunu, where young Rolihlahla would spend much of his childhood. Here he played with his sisters in the shade of the trees and, when he was a little older, began to follow his older brothers, playing the games that they played, with sticks and stones and oxen made from clay. These were happy days for little Rolihlahla.

When he was older, Rolihlahla followed his brothers and cousins into the green hills that surrounded their family home, driving the family's oxen to new pastures. There the young herdboys took good care of the livestock, leading them to fresh water and guarding them against danger. It was here too that the boys learned to play the traditional games of the Xhosa people, practising the stick-fighting they had seen the older boys perform with such skill. Rolihlahla's youth was a traditional one, a time spent playing and working with his brothers, sisters and cousins and learning the skills required of a boy in rural Transkei.

When Rolihlahla was seven years old he was sent to school. Although he could no longer wander the hills with his brothers or play in the long grass with his sisters, he was excited to be at school. He longed to learn more about his ancestors and the story of his people. He knew that if he went to school and worked hard, his mother and father would be very proud. Not many boys his age went to school. So every day Rolihlahla would make his way to the mission school. Like many children at the mission schools at this time, this is where Rolihlahla was given the name Nelson because some of his white teachers struggled to say his Xhosa name. So it was that Rolihlahla Mandela became known as Nelson Rolihlahla Mandela.

Sadly, when Nelson was just nine years old, his father died, and the boy was taken from his family home in Qunu and placed in the care of Chief Jongintaba Dalindyebo of the Thembu people, who had agreed to look after the young boy. Nelson was very sad to lose his father. Hendry had been a strict but fair man, who took good care of all his children, and raised them well. But although Nelson missed his father, he was happy in his new home with Chief Jongintaba at The Great Place. Because Jongintaba was a chief, young Nelson lived in one of the biggest and grandest huts he had ever seen and quickly made many new friends among the children in the village.

The young Nelson Mandela loved school. He enjoyed learning about new things and different places, and he especially loved learning about people. He studied hard and did well at school. And then, at the age of 16, Nelson spent some time at a special initiation school, where the young boy became a man. Initiation is very important to the Xhosa people. All young boys are expected to go through circumcision and Nelson was no exception. He and the other boys gathered on the banks of the Mbashe River, where they lived alone during the initiation period. They sang and danced and, on the morning of the ceremony, they swam in the river and then wrapped themselves in special blankets. Once the ceremony was over, the young men covered their faces with white clay and then washed themselves in the water of the Mbashe. The boys had at last become men.

Soon after Nelson turned 16, he was sent to boarding school at a Methodist mission known as Clarkebury, which had been built on land his great-grandfather had given as a gift to the missionaries so that they could build a school. From Clarkebury, he moved on to college at Healdtown and then, when he graduated at the age of 21, to the South African Native College at Fort Hare, a well-known university where many important young black people had gone to study. While Nelson was at Fort Hare he met many young students just like him. They shared ideas and talked a lot about what it was like to be a black person in South Africa. They dreamed about a country where all people would be equal and everyone would be treated fairly. A few of these young men would later become leading members of black society and play important roles in the struggle for freedom.

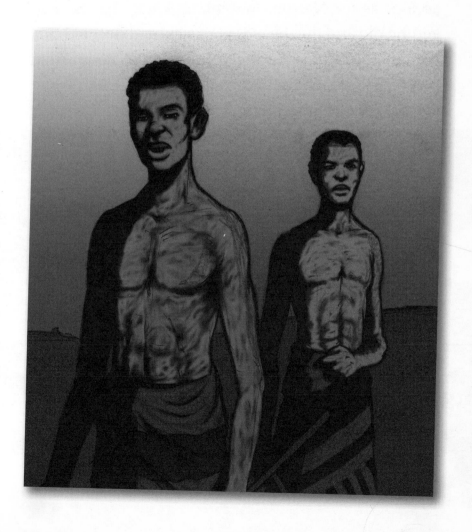

Nelson did not stay at Fort Hare very long. He was a stubborn young man, and after an argument with the principal, he returned to Chief Jongintaba's royal kraal at The Great Place and refused to go back to university. Of course, Jongintaba was not at all happy with the young man's decision and soon announced that he had found wives for his own son, Justice, as well as for Nelson. Jongintaba knew that he was getting old and that he was very sick, and decided that the time had come for the young men to be married and to settle down with a family.

But Justice and Nelson would not give up their freedom so easily. They felt that they were too young and not ready to take wives, so together they came up with a plan to run away to Johannesburg. There, they believed, they could find good jobs, earn some money and make their own decisions about their future. So it was that, in 1941, Nelson and Justice packed up their things and made their way to the big city.

As young men from rural Transkei, Nelson and Justice worried that they would not find work in Johannesburg and if Justice's father had not arranged a job for his son as a clerk at one of the mines, the young men may well have had to return home. Luckily, Justice was able to get Nelson a job, too, as a security guard at Crown Mines. But it wasn't long before Nelson began bragging that he had run away from home and had disobeyed the wishes of Chief Jongintaba. The people at the mine did not like the fact that Nelson had ignored the wishes of the chief, so they told him to leave. What would he do, alone and without a job in the big city? Then Walter Sisulu, one of Nelson's new friends, found him a job in a lawyer's office.

In 1943, once he had settled down in the city and in his new job, Mandela began studying law at the University of the Witwatersrand. This was a whole new world for the young man from the Transkei. The city was big and busy, full of people, rich and poor, bustling to and from their jobs, trying hard to earn a living so that they could send their children to school and make sure that they had something to eat. Mandela saw how hard life was for these people, and it was during this time that he became even more involved in the struggle for freedom for his fellow South Africans. Nelson was more determined than ever to see his people treated with fairness and dignity.

At the University of the Witwatersrand, just like he did back at Fort Hare, Mandela met and became friends with other South Africans who were fighting for equal rights for everyone. Many of his new friends were members of the African National Congress (ANC). He would go with them to political meetings and have long discussions about freedom and human rights. He even joined the Youth League, young members of the ANC who wanted to make their own contribution to the struggle. Together, Mandela and his friends would talk about how they could help the black people of South Africa. As a lawyer, Mandela knew that he could serve his people well, teaching them about their rights as workers and as South African citizens.

One day, while he was still studying at university and going to meetings and rallies in his spare time, he visited the home of his friend Walter Sisulu. Here he met Walter's beautiful but shy young cousin, Evelyn Mase, and the two fell in love. Mandela liked the young nurse's gentle smile and her strong belief in God. The time they spent together was filled with laughter, and in 1944 Nelson Mandela and Evelyn were married. Evelyn was a loving wife and Nelson a caring husband, and when Evelyn gave birth to Thembi, both parents were very proud of their baby boy. But Nelson and Evelyn's joy at starting their own

family turned to sadness nearly two years later when their new baby, a girl called Makaziwe, died. Nelson and Evelyn had two more children: another son, Makgatho, and another little girl, Makaziwe, who was named after her sister who had died. But life was not always easy for the young family. Much of Nelson and Evelyn's married life together was taken up by Nelson's devotion to his people and their struggle for freedom.

In 1948, white South Africans voted the National Party into government and the policy of apartheid was put into place. Lots of new rules and laws were

written so that the lives of all black South Africans became more and more difficult. Black people were told where they could live, where they could work, and even where they could walk. They needed special permission to be in white areas, and had to show a special book, called a pass, if a policeman or other government officer asked to see it. Black people were not free to do what they wanted to do in their own country. This was a very sad time for all black South Africans, and many black leaders were determined to put a stop to all these unfair laws.

By now Nelson had become a lawyer and, together with his friend Oliver Tambo, was helping other black people fight for justice in their communities. Mandela was already seen as an important leader in black politics and society, and this worried the new government. The white leaders did not like that the young black lawyer Nelson Mandela was so well loved and so respected by fellow black South Africans, so they watched him carefully. They saw how hard he fought to make sure that black people were treated fairly and with respect. They saw how he taught them to defend what they believed was right. It was clear that he was not afraid to stand up against the government. Soon the white government lost patience with the young lawyer and Mandela was banned and not allowed to appear in public as a leader of any kind.

In the early 1950s, the government stepped up its apartheid policies and made a number of laws that affected the lives of all black South Africans. These included, among many others, that black people were not allowed to marry white people, they had to live in separate areas, and could not vote in the same way that white South Africans could. In 1952, Mandela and his comrades started the Defiance Campaign. This campaign encouraged 'non-white' South Africans to break the apartheid laws. It meant that black people, for example, would travel in train coaches set aside for white people, they would stand in 'whites only' queues at banks, post offices and shops, and swim at 'whites only' beaches. The government was very angry, and immediately started arresting people who broke these laws, including Mandela. This was Mandela's first time in jail. As he sat in his dark, cold cell, he became even more determined to see his people set free. But the Defiance Campaign was a big success, and showed ordinary South Africans how powerful they could be if they all stood together against the race laws.

As matters in South Africa grew worse and worse, members of the ANC felt that they needed to do something to show the government how strong South Africans could be if they stood together in unity. So it was that in June 1955 thousands of people came together in Kliptown to show their support for a

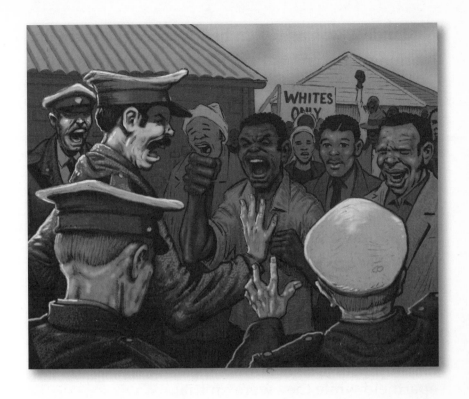

special document that had been drawn up to outline how black South Africans saw the future of their country. This important gathering became known as the Congress of the People and the document was the Freedom Charter. This public show of unity became a symbol of the struggle for freedom, but it made the government even more nervous about the possibility of black South Africans rising up in anger against apartheid. Mandela, one of the leaders, was banned and there were lots of arrests and police raids across the country as the government tried to stop more action.

Mandela was asleep in bed when, very early one morning in December 1956, there was a loud thumping at the front door. It was the police and they had come to search his home and arrest him. Mandela and 155 of his comrades, all arrested over the next 10 days, were taken off to the Johannesburg prison known as The Fort, where they were stripped naked, searched and then locked up. They were all charged with treason and put on trial. The legal process was a long one, and the court case, at the old Drill Hall, went on and on. This became known as the Treason Trial, and even though the political activists were allowed to go home every night, many of them, including Mandela, found it very difficult to continue with their struggle against apartheid while they were on trial.

While he was on trial, Mandela would spend most of the day in the courtroom at the Drill Hall and it was here, one day in 1957, that he met the beautiful young social worker Winnie Madikizela. Although Mandela was still married to Evelyn, their marriage was no longer a happy one. Because Mandela had become so involved in the struggle for freedom, the shy Evelyn found it difficult being his wife. After he was arrested for the first time, Mandela returned home to find that Evelyn had decided to move out and they were eventually divorced. So it was that, in June 1958, a year after he met Winnie, Mandela married her.

The young Winnie Mandela was not very active in politics, but she was devoted to her new husband. They were often seen together during the Treason Trial, the proud lawyer and activist holding the hand of his pretty young bride. Being married to such an important figure in the struggle, Winnie became more and more involved in the fight against apartheid, supporting her husband and sharing his dreams for a free and democratic South Africa.

During the years of apartheid, Winnie suffered the same punishments experienced by Mandela and his comrades in prison. She, too, was banned, imprisoned and even sent away to a dry dusty town in the Free State where the government felt she would do less damage in her own fight against apartheid.

On 21 March 1960, a group of people gathered in Sharpeville to protest against the pass laws that forced them to carry pass books and to explain why they were in 'white' areas. They carried posters and sang songs that told of their anger and their pain, but the police saw their peaceful marching as a danger. The policemen pulled out their weapons and shot into the crowds, killing 69 innocent people. News of the killings quickly

flashed across the country and around the world. It had become very clear to everyone that there would be war in South Africa if nothing was done about the hatred that was growing among its citizens. Mandela and his comrades immediately suggested that black leaders take a stand against the killings and the pass laws that continued to control the movement of black people in their own country by burning their pass books so that all could see. It wasn't long before the apartheid government declared a State of Emergency, which meant that police could arrest anyone they thought was a threat to the government. One of the first arrests was of Nelson Mandela, and in the next week the ANC and other political groups were banned.

Eventually, in August 1960, the State of Emergency was lifted and those comrades in court during the Treason Trial were allowed to go home. By this time, the ANC had become even stronger and was receiving a lot more attention overseas. This, of course, made the apartheid government even more nervous. It did not like the idea of black South Africans getting help from other countries in their struggle for equal rights, so it carefully watched the activities of Nelson Mandela and other black leaders. But Mandela and his comrades knew what was going on, so they secretly formed an organisation, which they called Umkhonto we Sizwe (which means 'Spear of the Nation'), that would help fight the evils of apartheid. The members of the organisation, including Mandela, also moved around often so that they could stay out of the way of the police and avoid being arrested. To be put into jail again meant that they would not be able to carry on with their struggle for freedom. Many hid away in safe houses or wore clever disguises. At one point, Mandela even grew a beard so that no one would recognise him as he went about his business.

During this time, the ANC and other black political groups became even more determined to tell the world, especially the people of Africa, about what was happening in South Africa and how black people were suffering. Mandela travelled across the

continent and even visited London to spread the word about the ANC and its fight for freedom. He also continued to study so that he and his comrades could learn how people in other countries, such as Russia and Cuba, fought for their freedom. Mandela even did some army training to learn how to fight, but while he was at an army camp in Ethiopia, he got news that he was needed back in his own country. He hurried back to Johannesburg, and there he pretended to be a gardener working at a house, known as Liliesleaf Farm, in the suburb of Rivonia. One day he was called to a meeting of ANC leaders in Durban, but on his way back, disguised as a chauffeur, the police spotted him and Nelson Mandela was arrested yet again.

During the trial following his arrest, Mandela acted as his own lawyer and arrived at the court in October 1962 wearing the traditional dress of a Xhosa prince. As he entered the packed courtroom, there was a gasp from the public who had come to see the great leader defend himself in a white court. Among the visitors to the trial were Mandela's mother, Fanny, and his young wife and their two daughters, Zindzi and Zeni. The children were very happy to see their father again, but were sad that he was facing another trial and, quite possibly, another jail sentence. The court officials were determined that this time Mandela would not be set free and, although he spoke well and presented a good argument, Nelson Mandela was sentenced to five years in jail for leaving the country without asking permission and for encouraging black workers to protest against their pay and working conditions.

Not long after Mandela was sent to jail, he heard about arrests that had taken place at the same Liliesleaf Farm where he had pretended to be a gardener while helping to organise the ANC and the struggle against apartheid. The house had been raided by police who had been watching it carefully after it was suspected to be a safe house for anti-apartheid activity. So when some of the top members of the ANC gathered at the Rivonia house to discuss the use of weapons against the apartheid system, the police stormed in and arrested a number of important leaders, including Walter Sisulu and Govan Mbeki (the father of Thabo Mbeki, who would many years later become president of South Africa), accusing the men of planning to blow up government buildings. At the house, the police found letters written by Mandela before he went to jail. So it was that the men found themselves in court yet again in what was to become known as the Rivonia Trial.

With the public following the happenings at court, it became clear that the men on trial would face a long time in jail and even possibly the death sentence.

When the sentence was read out, nearly a year after the men had been arrested, Mandela and his comrades were relieved that they faced a prison term rather than be hanged. The men were sent to Pretoria, but after only a few days they were handcuffed and moved to Robben Island. Locked away in cold, damp cells, the prisoners were lonely and faced terrible conditions. They had almost no pleasures, and were allowed only a few basic needs, such as soap and toothpaste. They received very few visitors and were forced to wear a uniform that left them cold and uncomfortable. It was a sad time for Mandela. Alone in his cell, he thought about his happy childhood, and worried about how his own children were coping

without their father.

The misery of those first few days in prison on Robben Island only seemed to get worse as Mandela and the other prisoners began to realise that they would be spending many years on the island, a long way from their family and friends. Life on the island was very hard, and all the prisoners were forced to work long hours in either the blazing hot sun or the cold and rain. Some took care of the prison garden, others had to sew or clean or cook, while others were forced to chop stones or work in the lime quarries on the island. Mandela had to do all of these jobs at some point during his many years on Robben Island.

The work on Robben Island was very hard, and many of the prisoners spent most of the day working outside. For a long time most prisoners were not even allowed to wear long pants, and were forced to work in the cold wind and rain wearing the shorts that

were part of the prison uniforms.

In the evenings, they would go back to their dimly lit cells. There they would play board games, read or study. They were allowed very few letters from friends and family at home, and even when they were, many of the letters had some of the words cut out by the prison guards so that the prisoners couldn't read them. The officials didn't want prisoners knowing too much about what was happening beyond the island. Luckily, the prisoners were allowed to study, and many of them used the opportunity to read as much as they could about science, religion, history and sometimes even politics. They learned a lot while they were in jail on the island and, because so many of the political activists would spend so much time together, they were able to share their knowledge and learning with each other.

Nelson Mandela and his friend and comrade Walter Sisulu quickly became the leaders of the prisoners. But being a leader did not mean that they were given any special privileges. In fact, they were treated just the same as all the others. Their letters from home were also checked by the guards, and they were allowed very few visits from their wives and children. For the men locked away from the real world, visits from family and friends were treasured, and they looked forward to every visit. Many considered these visits from their wives as the only contact they had with the world outside. But the visits were very short and, for much of the time they spent in jail, sometimes weeks or even months apart.

Like all the other prisoners, Nelson Mandela missed his family very much, especially his wife Winnie. They hadn't been married very long when he had been sent off to jail, and she had been left to raise their children alone. He kept a photograph of Winnie in his cell, where it stood on his bookshelf, along with his Bible and other books. Here he also kept the prized tomatoes he grew in the vegetable patch in the prison grounds, and even shared his vegetables with some of the warders.

Nelson Mandela was 46 years old when he was sent to jail on Robben Island, and because he had been sentenced to life in prison, many of his friends and comrades in South Africa and overseas were afraid that he would be a very old man when he was eventually released – if he was ever released at all. But after a few years in jail on the island, it was clear that he had become an important leader in the struggle against apartheid and was seen by many, both in South Africa and overseas, as the man who was most likely to be the country's first black leader. As a result, many fighters for freedom in South Africa felt that it was very important for Mandela to be freed as soon as possible – not only because he was facing a lifetime in jail for having fought for freedom for his people, but also because he needed to take his rightful place as the leader of a democratic South Africa. Many people across the world started to call for Mandela's release, organising marches, rallies and demonstrations demanding that he be freed so that he could continue the struggle. But the apartheid government refused to even think about that possibility, and Nelson Mandela was to remain in prison for a total of 27 years.

Then suddenly, in 1982, Mandela and three other prisoners, including Walter Sisulu, were called from their cells on Robben Island and marched off to the ferry waiting in the small harbour. The wind howled and the waves tossed the ferry about on the rough sea as the prisoners were taken back to Cape Town where they were locked up in Pollsmoor prison. Life was a little better at Pollsmoor. The four new prisoners shared a room for a while, and could read newspapers, watch television and listen to the radio. But they were still in jail, and conditions outside were getting worse. Black South Africans were still suffering terribly under the laws of apartheid, and they were beginning to show their anger more and more often. As a result, police and other apartheid officials were using a lot more force to try to stop what they called 'violent unrest'. But there was little Mandela and his comrades, locked away at Pollsmoor, could do to help.

But the move from Robben Island to Pollsmoor gave everyone a little hope that things may be about to change. Important government ministers began talking to Mandela, and it seemed that the government might be changing its mind.

Then, in 1988, Mandela's life changed yet again, when he was moved to the Victor Verster prison in Paarl, just outside Cape Town. Here he lived in a warder's house rather than a cell. He also had television, his own bathroom and a garden. Friends from Pollsmoor were even allowed to visit sometimes. It was becoming clear that the apartheid government was preparing to come to some sort of agreement with

Mandela and his comrades and some people said that it was even possible that the government was getting ready to free Nelson Mandela from prison.

For all those many South Africans who had suffered under apartheid for so long, as well as their friends and families overseas, it seemed that the dark days of the struggle were nearly over. Newspapers and television news ran story after story, all guessing when Mandela would be freed. Eventually, on 2 February 1990, South African president FW de Klerk announced in Parliament that all banned political organisations would be allowed and political prisoners were to be released. Nelson Mandela would be one of those prisoners who would be freed. There was great excitement right across the world, but no one was more excited than Mandela and his family. At last the day had come when they would be together again after 27 years apart. While the world rejoiced and South Africans got ready to welcome their leader home, Mandela packed his few belongings and prepared to walk out of the prison gates to a life of freedom once again. Then, on the morning of 11 February 1990, he walked out of Victor Verster prison hand in hand with his wife Winnie. Together they raised their arms as a salute to freedom, and the gates of the prison clanked shut behind them. Television cameras flashed, the crowds cheered and Nelson Mandela walked to freedom at last!

Mandela smiled broadly. Around him he could see green vineyards, heavy with grapes. Above him the hot summer sun beamed down from a bright blue sky. It felt good to be free. As hundreds of cameramen from around the world tried to take his picture, he was helped into a car and slowly they made their way to Cape Town where he would make his first public speech in nearly 30 years. As the car made its way through the streets of the city, Mandela looked up at Table Mountain. He had seen the mountain every day while he was on Robben Island, but this time he was not seeing it from across the sea. This time he wasn't separated from it by the blue and grey waters of Table Bay. This time he was standing right at its foot, on the balcony of City Hall, and crowded around him were thousands and thousands of well wishers who had come to welcome him. Standing next to some of his old friends and comrades, including Walter Sisulu, who had been freed earlier, Mandela stood up to speak to the thousands of people who had gathered on the parade ground in celebration, as well as millions of television viewers across the globe who watched as he waved.

One of the biggest celebrations was in Soweto, where Mandela once lived. The people of Soweto gave him a huge welcome, with thousands waving and dancing and cheering as he made his way through the streets. He was once again among the people who had

supported him through his many years in jail, and he was happy to be back home. While Mandela knew that there was still a lot of work to do before his people could be truly free, he also knew that together they had already done much. But there was some sadness too. Not long after he was set free, two of Mandela's dearest friends died. One was Chris Hani, a young man who had played an important role in the struggle against apartheid, who was murdered outside his home. The other was Oliver Tambo, Mandela's great friend and comrade, who was president of the ANC for many years, helping to tell the world about how black South Africans were suffering under apartheid.

Once he was free, Nelson Mandela began talking with the government about how he and all South Africans could move peacefully away from apartheid to a new future in which everyone was free. The country had been ruled by an apartheid government for nearly 50 years, but now it was time to set things right. Mandela made it clear that all South Africans, no matter what the colour of their skin, had to play a part in forming a new South Africa. Many people in

the country, as well as overseas, were worried that the important changes that were about to take place would result in fear among some South Africans. Some people did not want to see the country change at all, but many had waited so long for their freedom and the chance to vote for their own government that it soon became clear that South Africans of all races would work hard to make sure that the move to democracy would be happy and peaceful.

At last the day came when all South Africans were free to vote. On 27 April 1994, people of every colour, from every walk of life, made their way to voting stations all across the country. For many, this would be their first election, the very first time they were allowed to make a cross next to the picture of the person they wanted to see in government. The African sun baked down on long queues of smiling voters as they waited and waited for their special moment. Early in the day, Nelson Mandela had made his way to the voting station where he would cast his own vote and, with cameras flashing and hundreds of people watching and cheering, he smiled brightly and dropped his ballot note into the sealed box. When the election results were finally announced, there was much joy and celebration. The ANC had won, and Nelson Mandela was to be the country's first black president. This day had been South Africa's Freedom Day.

Just two weeks later, on 10 May 1994, Nelson Rolihlahla Mandela declared his loyalty to his people and his country as he was sworn in as the country's first democratically elected president. Standing in front of thousands of visitors to the Union Buildings in Tshwane, Mandela smiled and remembered how 30 years ago he had been sent to jail on Robben Island by the apartheid government. He remembered how he and his comrades had fought so long and so hard for the freedom of all South Africans. Again the cameras flashed and millions of people watched on television as the little boy from a tiny rural village, who had

given up much of his life in the fight for human rights, became president. Few people could imagine how difficult that job must have been, how much Mandela must have suffered over the years, separated from his friends and family for so long, but determined to set South Africa free. The party that followed was a joyful one, and when Mandela eventually turned out the light that night, he was so excited he could hardly sleep. It had been a long, tiring but exciting day for him and his people!

Being president was very different to being a prisoner. Instead of getting up early in the morning, when it was still dark, and eating cold porridge and dry bread from a tin plate, Mandela could get up whenever he wanted and he would be served hot breakfast on proper plates. But Mandela still got up early every day – to do his exercises, just like he did when he was in prison, and to make his own bed! He didn't like to sleep late, because he knew that there was lots of work to do. To be a good president, he had to do his duty. There were new laws and important decisions to be made. He had to help other leaders make sure that South Africans had proper homes, that they had enough to eat, and that they had access to medicine and a good education. He also had to meet presidents and princes, kings and movie stars, even pop singers and sports stars.

In 1995, when South Africa won the Rugby World Cup, Mandela handed the trophy to the team's proud captain wearing the green-and-gold jersey and cap of the Springbok team. But Mandela also had to deal with serious issues that affected the lives of all of his people. He wanted the world to know how HIV/Aids was killing people, so he travelled all over the country and across the world, talking about this terrible disease, teaching people about how they can avoid getting it and how they can treat it. He told everyone who would listen how much sadness the disease brings and explained that he, too, had experienced the pain of losing friends and family to HIV/Aids. Mandela was determined that one of the most important gifts he could give to the people of Africa, especially South Africa, was to teach them about HIV/Aids.

But even though the new president of South Africa met all sorts of important people and visited wonderful, faraway places, Mandela also made time to spend with his family. Although he and Winnie shared the same dreams for South Africa, they agreed that they no longer loved each other as they once did and, in 1996, they were divorced. But they made sure that they saw as much of their children and grandchildren as they could.

Mandela had spent far too many years away from his family, so even as president he would often visit

his son and daughters, as well as their own young children. He took great joy in being an ordinary father and grandfather, remembering his own happy childhood in rural Transkei.

On his trips around the country, President Mandela met many interesting people who he admired for the good work they were doing. One of those people was Graca Machel, the wife of Samora Machel, the president of Mozambique who had died in a plane crash in 1986. She was a kind, happy and generous woman, much loved by the people of Mozambique, where she continued to play an important role in the lives of her people. She and Mandela began to spend more and more time together and it soon became clear that they were falling in love. His eyes shone brightly whenever he was with her, and they would often hold hands and laugh together. And then, when Mandela turned 80 years old in 1998, he announced his marriage to his Graca. The people of South Africa were overjoyed that their president had found happiness with a charming new wife, and there was much celebration across the world.

With his new wife happily at his side, Mandela continued to lead his country and his people forward, but he had already begun to hand some of his duties to his deputy. And when the new elections took place in 1999, it was no surprise that Thabo Mbeki became

the next president of South Africa. Although he had
to work hard to continue the job started by Mandela,
Mbeki had worked side by side with the president
for a long time and Mandela was sure that he could
retire knowing that the country was in good hands.
But even though Mandela was no longer president,
he continued to work as much as he could. He offered
advice when he was asked, visited Aids patients
in hospital, travelled overseas to meet with other
important leaders and welcomed visitors to South
Africa, encouraging them to help bring about even
more changes in a country that was continuing to grow.

There came a time, though, that Madiba began to enjoy a more private life too. By the time he turned 90 in 2008, he was able to relax, visit with his family and think back on all he had done for his country and his people. Nelson Mandela had been a farm boy, a lawyer, a leader, a husband, a father, a grandfather, but most of all, he had been a hero.